oms
on the
mo

Practical Solutions for Busy Lives

(family vacations made simple)

BARBOUR
PUBLISHING

Published by Barbour Publishing, Inc., P.O. Box 719, Uhrichsville, Ohio 44683
www.barbourbooks.com

Our mission is to publish and distribute inspirational products offering exceptional value and biblical encouragement to the masses.

Member of the
Evangelical Christian
Publishers Association

Printed in China.
5 4 3 2 1

Contents

Introduction

My parents were conscientious about making our long, annual car trip vacations educational. Whenever we saw a sign alerting us that a "historical marker" would soon be visible beside the road, my father would direct the passengers on the appropriate side of the car to read the marker—as we passed by at an only slightly decreased speed. As the marker rapidly vanished in the distance, he would always ask, "So, what did it say?" We soon renamed these roadside trivia signs *hysterical markers*.

To this day, some of the best times I remember from my childhood relate to family trips and vacations. Do you yearn for time to really work on family relationships? Getting away from the pressures of everyday life makes it easier to focus on one another. Sadly, travel anxiety and planning paranoia keep many parents from using their time off to create such enduring memories.

There's no need to get hysterical about a family vacation. You will have to spend some time in advance planning, but that preparation pays big dividends in making travel easier and more fun. Planning is what makes family trips simple, but the key to a memorable vacation is in your attitude. Many times it's not where you go or what you see, but the feeling of closeness and cooperation your family experiences. Whether you are cruising the Caribbean or escaping a water-logged tent in the middle of the night, make the best of your time together now and happily reminisce for a lifetime!

THE
AMUSEMENT
PARK

The Amusement Park

It's every child's dream trip—loop-the-loops, hair-raising drops, and animated characters come to life. Everywhere you turn at an amusement park, a new attraction looms to entice, amaze, and excite your child, and the child in you!

Amusement park complexes may offer special opening and closing times for visitors staying at an affiliated resort. Take advantage of these opportunities to go on popular rides while there are fewer people in the park. The most fun evening of one family trip to Disney World was thanks to a special program that allowed us to visit selected areas of the Magic Kingdom from ten o'clock to twelve o'clock at night, after the rest of the day's crowd had left. We used that time for unlimited turns on the most popular, and usually most crowded, rides and returned the next day to see other attractions.

If you're planning on visiting an amusement park outside of the summer months, be sure to call to check on ride availability. Even if the park is open, some popular rides may be closed for maintenance. Opening and closing times are usually closer together as well.

Good IDEA

If you'll be staying for a few days, plan on taking afternoon breaks. Return to the hotel for a nap or a swim, or rest your feet at an air-conditioned show in the park.

Items Needed:

- Sunscreen
- Lightweight rain ponchos
- Camera
- Small snacks and bottled water (if permitted)

Most amusement parks, including the "mega" parks in Florida and California, wisely separate their rides and attractions into sections to accommodate kids of different ages and heights. If your family includes a wide variety of ages, it may be best for adults to divide up with kids and set a place and time to periodically regroup. Losing a family member in a large amusement park setting is one of a parent's biggest fears. Use these five tips to help keep track of everyone:

1. Buy each member of your group the same brightly colored shirt or hat to wear in the park.

2. To get your attention more quickly, teach very young children to call out your given name if they can't see you instead of "Mommy."

3. Train kids never to go away with someone unless he or she knows your family "password"—even if that person says you are hurt.

4. When you arrive at the park, point out a place for your children to meet you should they become lost.

5. Be sure to have current photos of your children in your wallet or backpack to show around if you become separated.

Travel guides like *The Unofficial Guide to Walt Disney World 2004* by Bob Sehlinger (John Wiley and Sons, Inc.), give excellent information on how to make the most of your trip. If you're unsure how your early elementary-schooler will handle the Tower of Terror, travel guides also rate the scare factor, or comfort, of rides for preschoolers up through senior citizens.

Kids Can Too!

Look at a map of the park and let your child choose which section to visit first, second, and third.

Don't feel like you have to travel to a large theme park to enjoy the experience. Kids are often just as thrilled with a trip to a local amusement park (individually owned and operated versus a large, corporate franchise). The smaller-scale park near our home offers as many rides as we can comfortably tackle in a day. However, there is one caveat to small parks: Even if day passes are available, some special rides and attractions may cost extra. (One price does not always cover all!)

Cost Savers

Most park passes are expensive, but discounts on tickets can often be found at local grocery stores or banks. Parks occasionally offer lower ticket prices in connection with advertising promotions on products. (For example, bring in an empty can of a certain brand of soda and get money off your entry fee.)

Make It Memorable

another **g r e a t** *trip*

If you are planning a trip to a Disney property, one of the best souvenirs to bring home is an autograph book filled with signatures from the Disney characters you find as you go around the park. On the facing page, attach a photo taken of your child with the character to make the book extra-special. Try to reserve spots at a character "meal" in the park or at a resort to get several autographs at one time without a long line.

MOM Meditations

"Anyone who will not receive the kingdom of God like a little child will never enter it" (Luke 18:17). When was the last time you practiced having a childlike heart? Enjoying things on a child's level helps us rediscover that childlike part of ourselves that God longs to touch.

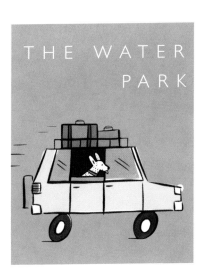

THE WATER
PARK

The Water Park

Looking for some good clean fun? Whether your family enjoys the slipping, sliding thrills of a water slide (think rollercoaster on water) or the relaxation of a river float, water parks offer a wet 'n' wild adventure. While you may think of a trip to a water park as a great way to beat the heat, indoor parks are opening up in parts of the country with cold winter weather, like the Wisconsin Dells, for year-round fun.

As with amusement parks, many water park rides or slides have height restrictions, but a "kiddie" area is usually available where younger guests climb, slide, and paddle around under your supervision. Often you can pay more for your own personal inner tube or mat to use on the larger slides. While generic park tubes are usually available, the supply is limited. On days when the park is busy, you can spend a lot of time trying to snag an unused tube, so paying extra for your own may be worthwhile.

Word to the Wise: Know what swimsuits your children will be wearing and think of ways to create an identifiable mark, such as a zinc sunscreen shape on the shoulder, so you can easily pick them out of a crowd.

Arrive early to beat the crowds, and visit the big, popular rides first. When the lines begin to get long, take a break in the wave pool or float down the lazy river. Another good time to try the big rides is during lunch, so you might want to take your own meal either earlier or later than usual.

Items Needed:

- Towels
- Sunscreen
- Goggles for the wave pool
- Water wings for small children
- Ear drops (helps avoid swimmer's ear)
- Dry clothes for the ride home
- Wear water shoes or water socks in the park, if you have them, because the concrete in between attractions can get very hot. They also help protect your feet from burns and scrapes as you go down the slides.

Good IDEA

For maximum protection from the sun, apply sunscreen before you drive to the park and *at least* once while there. (Before eating lunch is a good time.)

great another trip

$ Cost Savers

Call and ask if the water park allows you to bring in your own food and drinks in a cooler (no glass). You'll eat better and save money!

The Historical Trip

Adults appreciate the importance of connecting with our common national history, but kids are often less than enthusiastic about the prospect of a vacation spent visiting battlefields, museums, and homes of historical figures. Try telling your children that your next trip will be spent imagining the sights, sounds, and emotions of the Civil War while driving around Gettysburg, Pennsylvania—and watch them roll their eyes.

You'll obtain the highest level of interest and cooperation from kids by asking for input on what they'd like to see and tying your trip to subjects they are familiar with—like those they have discussed in school. Look at a map and group together several historical venues that are in close geographic proximity. (For example, Gettysburg and Philadelphia, Pennsylvania, and Washington, D.C.)

For information on sites of interest, contact the tourism department of the state you will be visiting by calling their toll-free number (see Appendix A); or check out their Web site by typing in www.state.—.us, where the dash is replaced by the two letter abbreviation you use for a state when addressing a letter.

Word to the Wise: Take advantage of city or state visitor information centers when you arrive. The staff there can lend firsthand experience as to which attractions would most interest your family.

Where to Stay

Historical vacations offer several different choices for where to stay. If you know you'll be spending most of your time out sightseeing, the size and luxury of the room is not as important. Economize by reserving a smaller room or one that is located a distance away from the tourist area. However, there are several instances when it makes sense to spend extra on your accommodations. If most of the sites of interest are located downtown, you will save on gas, parking, and time in traffic by spending more on a room close by and walking. Your family may also want to splurge by staying the night in a historic inn or bed and breakfast. This type of accommodation can be memorable but also costs more than a regular hotel. (Children are not always welcome, either!)

Cost Savers

Hotels in historical areas often have differing rate structures depending on the season of year. The most expensive season is usually during the summer months, so you can save on where you stay by traveling at an off-peak time of year.

Scheduling major sightseeing excursions for the morning is a good idea. Parents, kids, and tour guides are fresher—and often attendance is lighter.

Do allow for breaks during the day. Few children, or adults for that matter, have the attention span for a full day of history! Save blocks of relaxation time for the afternoon. Encourage good behavior while you are sightseeing by planning a special activity for kids to look forward to later. This is a vacation, so take time to swim in the pool or treat everyone to an ice cream sundae!

Fun *historical* excursions

- Visiting a wax museum
- "Panning" for gold or gems
- Touring a working grist mill (get some cornmeal to make cornbread at home)
- Dressing up in period costumes at a "dressing salon"

Good IDEA

Pack your day pack or purse thoughtfully; many historical sites now have security checkpoints and some items are not allowed through.

Souvenir Ideas:

- Books on famous people and the places you visit. (We even found a recounting of one Gettysburg battle illustrated in comic book style for our early reader!)

- "Antique" games and toys like wooden cars or rag dolls

- Collect postcards from the sites you visit and have your child write their remembrances on the back to create a postcard journal of the trip.

- Old-fashioned candy—a good reward for cooperative behavior

- Videos and DVDs about historical events

- Costumes of the time like prairie bonnets or coonskin caps. Be aware that items like pop guns, rubber band guns, and swords figure prominently in most historical gift shops. If you do not want to purchase these types of items for your children, discuss your policy with them before the trip.

Make It Memorable

History comes alive for kids when they have the opportunity to experience it for themselves. Make reservations to sample the food of the time at a "period" restaurant. Include a visit to the reconstruction of an old town where you can see things in operation from the old days like a blacksmith shop.

Kids Can Too!

Before you travel, collect brochures and guidebooks in an expandable file. Ask your children to play tour guide and read out loud the history and descriptions of what they will see as you travel to a site.

MOM Meditations

"Remember the days of old; consider the generations long past. Ask your father and he will tell you, your elders, and they will explain to you" (Deuteronomy 32:7). Instead of telling the Israelites to remember their checkered past so they would not repeat it, Moses is reminding them of the Lord's past deliverance and answer to prayer. Think about your own past. When have you felt the touch of God's healing hand or His saving grace?

From the Trip files

One thing you do a lot of on a historical vacation is *walk.* On the last day of our trip to Washington, D.C., my husband and I had to resort to a small fib to get our kids to go the "extra mile." After spending the morning touring the Smithsonian Museum of Natural History, we convinced everyone to walk down to the Washington Monument with encouraging comments like, "It's just down there. See it?" As we walked, we got the kids to promise to accompany us the extra distance "just past the hill" to the Lincoln Memorial—our real destination, being from the land of Lincoln. They were ready to give up once we reached the top of the hill and saw how far we still had to go to reach our goal. Only the inspiring beauty of the memorial, and piggyback rides for the younger children, got us the rest of the way. The unrelenting whining on the walk back to the subway reminded me that my definition of *a lot* of walking differs dramatically from my kids'!

THE
ADVENTURE
VACATION

The Adventure Vacation

Adventure vacations cater to the adrenaline craving in many of us. If your family enjoys the excitement of the unconventional, going whitewater rafting, bicycle touring, or horseback riding may make a memorable getaway. There are two keys to an enjoyable adventure vacation: finding a reputable company with experience and having good luck with your weather.

The best souvenirs from an adventure vacation are pictures, which may mean bringing a disposable, waterproof camera along. It's also fun to buy items you can use on your trip like hats or cords to hold glasses or sunglasses on your head.

Word to the Wise: Be aware of your family's adventure "level." Many trip outfitters will wonder about your level of prior participation or expertise.

Collect brochures from adventure "outfitters," and then do some research. Look for companies that offer *family* trips. Recommendations from families who have already had a similar adventure can give you a good place to start. Write down a list of questions like these to ask when you call, so you can compare answers between companies.

- How long have you been in business?

- How many people do you have on staff (versus a one-man operation)?

- What kind of variety is there in the trips you offer?

Moms
on the
Move

Ask what the weather and conditions are usually like at the time of year you'll be traveling. Current and historical weather information is also available on The Weather Channel's Web site: www.weather.com.

Click on the site's "vacation planner" link, and by typing in the city and state (or country) you'd like to visit, you'll get information on average monthly temperatures and precipitation.

Whitewater
RAFTING

- Water levels at various times of the year affect the difficulty of navigating the river. Directly after the spring thaw or during the rainy season, water levels are usually higher and there are more rapids. At the end of summer, water levels are generally lower, so the trip will take longer with fewer rapids.

- Your guide's river experience is more important for your safety than the abilities of the other rafters. Depending on the difficulty level of your trip, you may not need to be an experienced paddler or even an accomplished swimmer. However, many companies do have minimum age recommendations.

- If you don't like cold water, ask if the outfitter provides wetsuits or rain suits for the trip.

Kids Can Too!

If you question how your child will handle an adventure vacation, first try the activity on a smaller scale. Take him or her for a short trail ride at a nearby stable. Go canoeing on a local lake. Venture out on a four-hour bike ride that includes a picnic lunch.

Travel IDEA

Find out if your outfitter is a member of the United States Tour Operators' Association (USTOA), which offers a consumer protection plan. Check www.USTOA.com for a list of association members. If your outfitter is not listed, ask a travel agent if they are legitimate.

27

Bicycle TOURING

- Spend time going on long bike rides together before your trip. In addition to getting in shape, this will lessen "seat soreness."

- Consider the type of terrain you'll be riding over when choosing how long a trip you will take. Thirty miles a day may not seem like too much when you're riding on flat ground, but add some hills and the trip becomes much more challenging.

- For variety, pick a tour that intersperses riding days with days off to hike or sightsee.

- Invest in some biking gear like padded biking shorts, padded biking gloves, a roomy fanny pack to carry necessities, and a rain suit.

- Ask the touring company what kinds of bikes are available, including bike carts for little children, and if they provide helmets and water bottles.

- Many states offer do-it-yourself bicycle tours. In the Midwest, old railway lines have been removed and converted into bicycle/hiking trails. Some areas even supply names of individuals who will transport you and your bike(s) to the beginning of the trail (your vehicle awaits you at the trail's end) so you can ride the entire length without having to double back. Look for bike trail brochures at the state's visitor and information center or with other tourism brochures at a hotel.

another great trip

Horseback RIDING

- If you have younger children who would like to ride, inquire about minimum age restrictions (often eight years of age). Also ask if smaller-sized mounts and saddles are available—this can make a world of difference in your child's comfort and confidence level on the trip.

- Morning rides are preferable because the horses have more energy and there's a higher likelihood of seeing other wildlife along the trail.

- If you have a child who is very sensitive to smells, prepare him or her ahead of time. As one of our children noted, horseback riding can be a stinky business!

- Arrive early so the guides have plenty of time to match your size and riding ability to a horse.

- Being "saddle sore" is not an imaginary ailment! Even if you rode horses in your youth, it's wise to start off with a ride that only takes several hours. Don't sign on for a full-day trip until you're sure your backside and your knees can handle it.

- Wear blue jeans to avoid chafing and scratches from bushes and sturdy shoes, preferably with a hard sole. Bring bug spray to ward off flies.

- Horses can be spooked by clothing that flutters and gear that bumps or pokes them. Think "compact" when choosing which clothes to wear and which accessories to bring (no long scarves, big backpacks, or things hanging from belts).

- Don't be shy about asking to change places in line if your horse has difficulty getting along with its neighbors.

THE CAMPING TRIP

The Camping Trip

Families fall into two categories—those that love camping and those that consider "camping out" to be a night spent in a hotel without a pool. If you haven't tried communing with the great outdoors or are unsure how your family members will enjoy the experience, rent or borrow some equipment to "try before you buy." Take a day trip to the campground before your overnighter and scout out good sites (mark them on a site map for future reference). Campgrounds usually allow reservations for a portion of their sites, so you can stop by the office and put down a deposit in advance.

Word to the Wise: A good campsite is one that is level, with good drainage, and not right next to the bathroom—too much noise.

What to Bring

The easiest way to pack clothes, towels, and personal belongings is to use individual duffle bags. They're easy to shove in small spaces and encourage kids to be responsible for their own stuff. Each camper should bring several pairs of shoes: sneakers or boots for hiking, another pair to wear around the campsite in case the first gets wet or muddy, and a pair of plastic flip-flops or sandals to wear in the communal shower. A plastic cleaning caddy or bucket makes a great carrier for everyone's bath items like soap, shampoo, lotion, toothbrush, and toothpaste (punch small holes in the bottom for drainage).

Bring along a quiet evening activity to help everyone relax and get ready for bed. Our whole family enjoys listening to books on tape or CD before going to sleep. The combination of unusual night noises (including noisy neighbors) and stuffy air in the tent or camper can make sleeping difficult, too. Older preteens and teenagers may enjoy the novelty of their own separate tent, and you'll appreciate the lack of giggling and the privacy this arrangement affords.

Good IDEA

Most improved campsites have picnic tables. Bring a large screened cabin or tent to put over the picnic table so you can eat outside with fewer bothersome bugs. Add a lantern, and this also makes a great place to sit and talk or play cards in the evening.

Here is a list of general items to bring along—you'll want to customize this basic list to fit the time of year and your family's mode of camping. Garage sales are the most economical places to find supplies like cookware, plates, utensils, linens, and towels. There's no need to worry about finding matching sets, and things are easily replaced if ruined or broken.

- Sleeping bags and pillows (optional: cots or mattress pads)
- Bath towels, washcloths, dish towels
- Lanterns and flashlights with extra fuel and batteries
- Cookstove or small grill with extra fuel or charcoal
- Small tool kit
- Swiss Army knife
- Rope or twine

- Cookware and utensils
- Plates, cups, and silverware
- Two coolers (one for beverages, one for food)
- Clothes and personal toiletries
- Kitchen accessories: timer, grater, can and bottle openers, resealable plastic bags, aluminum foil, pot holders, paper towels, cutting board, vinyl tablecloth, matches or a lighter, dish soap, trash bags
- Bottled water
- First-aid kit
- Bug spray

On camping trips, we try to make do with as little as possible. As with most travel experiences, however, the fun is in the details. If you have the space, try packing some of these extra items:

- Star chart for locating planets and constellations
- Skewers or unpainted clothes hangers for roasting marshmallows
- Small plastic box to hold natural treasures found on walks
- Scooters or other riding toys to make trips to the bathroom easier
- Squirt bottles for water fights
- Binoculars

Kids Can Too!

It's amazing how readily kids will help with chores like setting the table, washing the dishes, and taking out the trash when they're out camping. A camping trip should be a break for you, too, so don't be shy about assigning everyone a job. You can even make up a rotating chore chart before you go.

Make It Memorable

We have a camping tradition of putting on a family talent show in the evenings around the campfire. The kids have told stories, sung songs, produced short plays, and even put on a yo-yo demonstration for their parents. They look forward to planning the evening's entertainment and start working on their "talent" around dinnertime.

another great trip

MOM Meditations

The nomadic people of the Old Testament lived in tents. In fact, part of a man's wealth was determined by how many tents he owned. The next time you're struggling with tent poles, consider the wealth in love and connectedness this family time together brings.

From the Trip files

My children's most memorable camping experience came on a campout with my parents. The kids and I were to spend the night in my family's ancient tent, while Grandma and Grandpa stayed in a nearby screened-in cabin. About three in the morning, a noisy thunderclap awoke everyone and announced the beginning of a torrential rainstorm. In no time, there was a small stream running through our tent. Despite the downpour, the kids and I decided to make a break for the relative safety of the cabin. We waited out the storm snacking and playing games. Even though we decided to call it quits in the morning—and spent a soggy couple of hours packing up the car—we remember this rainy overnight as one of our most amusing adventures.

THE

BEACH OR

LAKE HOUSE

The Beach or
Lake House

There's something about being around water that is
soothing. Listening to the waves, taking walks by the
shore, watching fish swim around the dock and birds fly over the water
adds up to a relaxing vacation—but then you remember, what about
the kids? The first couple of days they'll find these activities engaging;
then boredom (and the accompanying whining) can set in. To keep a
week-long trip to a beach or lake house interesting, it's important to
stay in an area with other activities and attractions nearby.

It's wise to make reservations in a place with as many alternatives
as possible in case water conditions or the weather don't
cooperate. Check out the local museums, zoos, or parks. A local
movie theater can drive away the blues on a rainy afternoon.

Word to the Wise: Sunrises and sunsets on the beach are often
the most intense displays of God's artistry. Take the opportunity
to enjoy them with your children.

To keep sun exposure to a minimum, get out on the water early, and then insist that everyone stay inside for a "siesta" after lunch. (The sun's rays are at their strongest between 10:00 A.M. and 2:00 P.M.) Play games, read, do crafts, or go sightseeing during peak sun hours. Remember that you *can* get sunburned on cloudy days—don't go out without an application of sunscreen. Put up a sun shelter on the beach (a tent with a top but no sides), so you can build sand castles, bury other family members, and watch the waves without sitting directly in the sun. Even then you'll need sunscreen to block rays reflecting off the sand and water.

IDEA

One of our favorite indoor activities at the beach is putting together puzzles. We even bring an old card table that we dedicate to the assembly of our latest 1,000-piece picture. Working over a puzzle provides lots of opportunities to talk and laugh together.

39

The best beach souvenirs have something to do with shells. When you get home, use the shells and small pieces of driftwood you collected to make a mobile or to fill up the base of a mason jar lamp. Glue the prettiest flat shells around a picture frame or small mirror. Fishermen may enjoy a shadowbox filled with their favorite lures (for safety you can first cut off the hooks with wire cutters).

Plan some activities specific to the beach or lake like:

- Going fishing—young children may not even need a fishing license.

- Eating something different—we have a beach tradition of visiting a local shop to buy fresh crab and shrimp caught that day. For dinner, everyone enjoys an old-fashioned seafood boil where the crab and shrimp are cooked, drained, and dumped out on a table covered with newspaper along with small boiled potatoes and ears of corn.

- Renting a boat for the day—a boat provides a different view of the water and the shoreline.

Make It Memorable

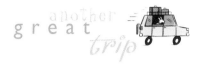

another
great
trip

If you can find a sand dollar, tell your child the "legend" of this unusual shell.

There are four holes along the edge of the sand dollar that some say stand for the four nails used at the crucifixion, and a fifth hole near the middle like the one made by the spear. On one side of the sand dollar is the shape of an Easter lily, on the other a Christmas poinsettia. If you break a sand dollar in half, little pieces in the shapes of doves come out of the center to spread good-will and peace.

MOM Meditations

"He got up, rebuked the wind and said to the waves, 'Quiet! Be still!' Then the wind died down and it was completely calm" (Mark 4:39). Vacation should be a time to calm our souls. If you've provided a place and props for the kids to entertain themselves, take a well-deserved break to "be still."

From the  Trip files

One year we arrived at the beach to find that a "scourge of the sea"—reminiscent of an Old Testament plague—had swept through the waters nearby, killing enormous amounts of seaweed. The tide pushed the dead seaweed into piles about one foot high all along the water's edge. Our kids took one look at that seaweed and said, "No way!"

Unfortunately, we had rented the beach house for a week, nonrefundable, of course. Determined that a little ocean flora would not ruin our vacation, my husband and I coaxed our children into the water, but even the adults couldn't stand the scratchy seaweed floating up against us on its way to the beach.

Thank goodness the beach house we rented was close to a water slide and a ferry ride away from Galveston, Texas, which has a train museum, an old-fashioned ice cream parlor and candy store, a rain forest habitat and million-gallon aquarium, and seashell shops. We had a great time—despite "the scourge!"

THE

FAMILY

VISIT

The Family Visit

Many of us live far enough away from extended family that their homes become frequent travel destinations. Older children—including parents—usually enjoy the opportunity to be doted on by grandparents, to reintroduce themselves to aunts and uncles, and to play with cousins. Younger children, however, may feel anxious about interacting with family members they barely know.

Spend some time before you go looking through pictures and sharing stories about the family members that kids will meet. One excited set of grandparents mailed "preview" photos of their house, including the rooms where everyone would stay, and a welcoming picture of them waving from the front steps! Put together a small photo album your child can bring along on the trip, and leave room in the back for new photos taken during the visit.

Word to the Wise: A special item from your or your husband's past that stays at Grandma's house can help acclimate a child quickly and be an important opportunity for sharing memories.

Bringing along some necessities from home can make your family more comfortable in another house. Consider packing these items if you have room, or pick them up after you arrive.

Items Needed:

- Childproofing materials like outlet covers and baby gates
- Nightlight
- Baby monitor or walkie-talkies
- Pillow, sleeping bag, and air mattress if there aren't enough beds
- Favorite food items for picky eaters

Do your own checking to make sure that medications, sharp utensils, and cleaning products are safely locked away.

Good IDEA

If you will be seeing elderly relatives, acquaint kids with their special needs. Discuss equipment they may see like wheelchairs or walkers. Explain that people may speak louder because of hearing impairments or that their speech may not always be clear and coherent.

Rules at relatives' houses can be stricter—or more lenient. Discuss "limits" with the adults of the house *before* a visit if you think they might be a problem. Ask your host or hostess to take the kids on a tour and explain the house rules shortly after you arrive. Remind everyone that cleaning up their own messes will help keep the peace.

Kids Can Too!

Ask kids to play reporter and interview their relatives. They can either write down family stories and history or record them on audio or videotape.

Relatives are a storehouse of information. Suggest that your host(s) pass along a favorite hobby or skill:

- Ask them to involve your child in the planning and preparation of a meal using a "family recipe."

- Have an uncle or grandfather take a child to the garage and help them make or fix something simple.

- Work in the garden together.

- Sew something by hand or on a machine. Teach kids how to crochet or knit.

A house can quickly feel over-crowded when one family visits another, so plan outings to avoid feeling cramped. Since most "natives" do not take advantage of attractions available in their hometown, take your hosts out sightseeing or for dinner. If you would like to go out alone with your spouse or with friends, ask your relatives if they would be willing to baby-sit—don't assume, and don't take advantage of their generosity (these are definite goodwill busters).

Make It Memorable

When you travel to see relatives, make a tradition of doing something that everyone enjoys, like going out to a special restaurant or spending time at a favorite park. Kids will look forward to this activity each time you visit.

MOM Meditations

Going home isn't the same after you have children. For one thing, your parents hurry out to hug their grandkids first instead of you! Help children understand that you want some one-on-one adult time with your relations once everyone gets settled.

THE CAR
TRIP

The Car Trip

Classic car trips are among our family's favorites because they offer so much flexibility in where you stop and what you see along the way. From lunch at a "Root Beer Saloon" (root beer on tap, no alcoholic beverages) to taking a cave tour by boat on an underground lake, we've had some of our most interesting and memorable experiences when we've turned off the highway.

The best car trip souvenirs are things kids can play with when they get back in the car like stuffed animals, miniature figures, Viewmaster slides, reading material, or Polaroid photos of sites you just visited. Have children decorate "memory boxes" before your trip so they'll have something to put these treasures in along the way.

Word to the Wise: Car trips are more enjoyable if you make the time for frequent breaks so everyone can stretch their legs. Plan your route so there are interesting stops at various intervals...

Several book series are available for those who enjoy impromptu detours off the beaten path:

- The "oddball" series, as in *Oddball Illinois: A Guide to Some Really Strange Places* by Jerome Pohlen, is published by Chicago Review Press and features books on at least six states—Illinois, Wisconsin, Indiana, Colorado, Minnesota, and Florida.

- The *Off the Beaten Path: A Guide to Unique Places* (Globe Pequot Press) series covers at least 35 states; each travel guide is written by a different author.

- The *Fun with the Family: Hundreds of Ideas for Day Trips with the Kids* (Globe Pequot Press) series also covers at least 32 states from Alabama to Wisconsin.

Good IDEA

Keep an outdoor play bag in the car so everyone can burn off some energy when you picnic or make a rest stop. Things to include: different types and sizes of balls (especially those you can inflate), Frisbee, bubbles, sidewalk chalk, and a jump rope.

Most parents are aware of the importance of "buckling up" in the car with an appropriate safety belt or car seat, but using a child's car seat *correctly* makes a big difference. Any restraint system may not protect your child in a crash if it is used improperly. For specific information about installing your car seat, consult a Child Passenger Safety (CPS) technician certified by the American Automobile Association (AAA). A list of certified CPS technicians is available by state or ZIP code at:

www.nhtsa.dot.gov/people/injury/childps/contacts/index.cfm

> Concerned about car seat recalls? The Auto Safety Hot Line provides current information on recalls: 888/327-4236 from 8 A.M. to 10 P.M. EST, Monday through Friday.

Before any trip, make sure your cell phone is charged and in the car and that you've put the following emergency items into an old diaper or duffle bag and stowed it in your trunk.

Items Needed:

- Work gloves
- Small tool kit
- Jumper cables
- Wheel chock
- Emergency flares
- Large flashlight with extra batteries
- Funnel
- Pocket knife or scissors
- Plastic jug of water
- Basic first-aid kit
- Nonperishable food (peanuts, dried fruit, granola bars)

Cost Savers

To save money on road trip entertainment, host a toy and book exchange with a couple of friends before vacation. Your kids can choose from a variety of new entertainment, without the expense.

Classic travel games and toys have more universal appeal than electronic toys. If you have trouble finding some of the car trip favorites from your childhood, look in a Cracker Barrel restaurant/store or a Restoration Hardware store or catalog for these:

* Travel bingo

* Magnetic games like checkers, chess, and backgammon

* Toy cars with a small plastic "town" mat (store in a lunchbox)

See Appendix B for more ideas of toys to bring.

Be sure to pack a supply of "surprise" toys to hand out when a major fight or meltdown seems imminent. Pick up these little toys on sale at discount stores whenever you shop. Some parents wrap them individually to open like presents; others simply fold them up in paper lunch sacks.

To minimize car clutter, store kids' stuff in plastic boxes with lids. These can also double as lap desks or game tables as needed. It may be easier for smaller children to keep toys in a toiletry bag hanging from the headrest of the seat in front of them. (This is one of those travel bags that you unfold and hang from a hook in the bathroom; they usually hold makeup and facial supplies.)

Keeping backseat bickering under control is a constant challenge. Try some of these techniques to maintain your sanity during a long day of driving:

- To handle complaints of "you're on my side," put a line down the middle of the backseat with masking tape.

- Tell kids before the trip that they will earn some predetermined reward for each half day of good behavior.

- Hand out four popsicle sticks (or more) to each child at the beginning of the day. You can designate each stick to be worth a quarter (or more). Every time a child argues, he has to return a popsicle stick to you. Upon reaching your destination, the kids are rewarded based on the number of sticks they still have.

- Periodically switch seats so that everyone gets a new view and a new partner.

- Ask your kids for their suggestions on how backseat bickering should be handled, and let them know you will enforce their decisions.

Kids Can Too!

Always pack a spiral notebook or diary and colored pencils (with sharpener) so your children can keep a travel diary. Ask them to record their daily thoughts and experiences and to include pictures or sketches of landmarks and animals they see along the way.

What's the worst illness your child can come down with on a car trip? Carsickness. There are some things you can do to help kids—and adults, for that matter—avoid this malady. One strategy is to avoid looking outside of the car, even if that means draping a towel or blanket over the window. Here are three additional driving don'ts:

- Don't allow your child to read, color, or play handheld games—this only makes the sensation worse.

- Don't let the inside car temperature become warm and stuffy. Leave a window open a crack for air circulation and to keep things on the cool side.

- Don't eat heavy, greasy meals, which can set off nausea, but don't ride on an empty stomach, either. Bring along light snacks to soothe your appetite.

- As much fun as traveling along winding back roads can be, staying on the highway may be safer for those prone to carsickness.

another great trip

MOM Meditations

One mom shared how, after the VCR in the van broke, her son accepted Christ on the long drive back from Colorado to Texas as the family spent time singing every hymn they could remember. Are you making the most of the time you and your family are spending together?

THE

CRUISE

The Cruise

Cruise lines recognize the desire of families to vacation together, and some are catering to parents traveling with children. The type of children's programs available and the age groups covered differ from cruise to cruise. According to my friend and travel agent, Disney and Carnival lines offer the most cruises tailored to kids. Often a family cruise may be centered around a theme, like "Camp Carnival" on Carnival cruise lines. A Disney cruise needs no further explanation! Other cruises offer activities geared toward older children, such as rock climbing walls, available on some Royal Caribbean cruise ships.

How do you choose where to go? Destinations in Mexico and the Caribbean are most popular with families. Wherever you visit, make sure there are interesting stops along the way with plenty of chances for sightseeing and other activities.

Word to the Wise: If you are the family photographer, ask other passengers to take family photographs with you in the picture, so years later kids won't ask "Where's Mom?"

Cruise package costs tend to be higher during the winter and summer months. You may find less expensive packages during the short break between seasons in April and May. Booking a cruise during hurricane season, July through early November, means you are taking chances with your vacation.

A cruise vacation is economical for many reasons:

- You only have to unpack once, yet you get to visit many different places.

- Meals are included. For those children with healthy appetites, this fact alone can yield big savings.

- Onboard activities and entertainment are generally free.

- It doesn't usually cost anything to disembark and walk around the beach or market at each stop. There are additional costs for special sightseeing excursions, snorkeling, and other activities off the boat.

- Dinner is often a dressy affair on a cruise, but you can get away with casual dress for the kids.

Even on the big ships, queasiness from seasickness can occur. Talk to your physician before saying "Bon Voyage" to ask about possible treatments. According to our physician, medication is available for children once they reach sixty to seventy pounds. For a nonchemical remedy, you can purchase wristbands that apply acupressure to points that supposedly decrease nausea.

Good IDEA

Consider taking out travel insurance on your trip—it's inexpensive and will save you lots of money if you must cancel due to medical illness or injury, inclement weather, or several other emergencies.

Kids Can Too!

Even young children can dress themselves, and in clothes that match, if you pack each day's complete set of clothing in separate, gallon-size plastic baggies.

another great trip

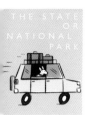

The State or National Park

State and national parks make excellent stopover points on any trip, as well as unique travel destinations for outdoor enthusiasts. Entertainment is readily available, with hiking and wildlife viewing topping the list.

The lodges and cabins available on many park properties are one of our best-kept secrets. Lodges usually feature rustic wilderness décor, including roaring fireplaces and restaurants with home-style cooking. Some have indoor pools and game rooms for the kids. Many of the lodges and cabins were built by the Civilian Conservation Corps (CCC) during the Depression era, so rooms are basic but spacious. Cabin amenities vary—from simple bedrooms with a bath to larger cabins complete with kitchenettes and living rooms. The cost of these accommodations is usually quite reasonable compared to hotels nearby—if there are any—but reservations can be hard to come by in some parks. National parks start taking reservations about a year in advance, so plan ahead!

Word to the Wise: The national parks in the United States contain amazingly beautiful and complex terrain. Trips like these offer an ideal chance for an outdoors science lesson.

Ideas for *Park Fun:*

- Hiking
- Horseback riding
- Wildlife viewing
- Hay rides
- Campfires
- Caving
- Swimming
- Storytelling
- Nature programs
- Boating
- Miniature golf
- Fish hatcheries

To find out more about parks in a particular area, contact the state(s) you will be visiting via the toll-free tourism numbers in Appendix A or on the Web. Information on national parks is available online at:

www.nps.gov

62

Make It Memorable

T-shirts make great park souvenirs and help support the park as well. For unique remembrances of your trip, buy toddler-sized T-shirts and sew up the arms and necks when you get home. Fill the T-shirts with pillow stuffing and sew up the bottoms. Your child can have a whole set of small pillows to remind him or her of your travels.

Day hikes are fun, healthy introductions to the wonders of nature. Be sure to investigate trail conditions and difficulty prior to setting out. Remember as you hike to turn back *before* getting too tired. Unless you are on a loop trail, you will have to walk back just as far as you came! It's more important to enjoy the scenery along the trail than to hurry along to a predetermined goal or view.

Kids Can Too!

Introduce your kids to the craft of orienteering—reaching an unfamiliar destination with a map and compass. Let them tell you which way the hiking trail leads by using an elevation map.

Long pants are appropriate hiking wear regardless of the season because they ward off scrapes, insect bites, and poison ivy. Hiking boots provide traction and help prevent ankle turns, especially in rocky terrain, but sturdy athletic shoes will work, too. Leave a clean change of clothes and shoes in the car for the end of the hike, in case your trail leads across a stream or mud puddle. Bring at least one day pack with these hiking necessities:

another
g r e a t trip

Items Needed:

- High-energy snacks like trail mix
- Bottles of water
- Bandanas (good for hot days and can double as a bandage)
- Small first-aid kit
- Hand or diaper wipes
- Insect repellent
- Sunscreen
- Moleskin or blister block bandages

Good IDEA

Before your trip, be sure to thoroughly break in whatever shoes you will be wearing to avoid painful blisters. One article on hiking suggested walking for at least twenty hours in new boots before using them on a long trek.

From the Trip files

The variety of activities available at most parks allows parents to spend one-on-one time with each child doing something that he or she enjoys. While at Petit Jean State Park in Arkansas, my eldest son and I snuck out before everyone else awoke to try out a difficult hiking trail. The waterfall at the end of the long stone stairway was beautiful, but it was not as rewarding as the feeling of accomplishment and camaraderie my son and I shared. At different times I've climbed fire towers and splashed through streams for the pleasure of uninterrupted conversation with a child. Walking in the woods together really does provide the best "getting to know you" time.

MOM Meditations

"Your faithfulness continues through all generations; you established the earth, and it endures" (Psalm 119:90). Visiting parks at different times of the year reminds us of God's faithfulness as we enjoy the changing of seasons. Just as spring always follows winter, we can rely on the Lord to be with us through all the seasons of our life.

THE SKI
RESORT

The Ski Resort

A ski vacation offers families the chance to romp in the snow and enjoy time outside together during the winter. The least expensive ski resort is usually the one closest to you, because travel and housing expenses are the biggest variables. Frequent skiers report that the prices of lift tickets and ski rentals do not differ greatly.

If your local terrain (Florida!) doesn't suit for a nearby ski vacation, investigate the cost of traveling to the bigger resorts and the periods of the season when it is more affordable to do so. Most resorts have detailed Web sites with a catalog of their rates throughout the season, information on ski schools, and resort amenities—an important factor for those in your family that may prefer the fireplace to the mountaintop.

Remember that safety comes first when you're skiing. Know your limits and your kids' limits, and love the journey!

Word to the Wise: Review a trail map—all resorts will have very detailed maps—as a family to plan where you will ski and meet up in case of separation.

Condominiums are popular housing choices, because making your own food saves time and money. Regardless of the type of accommodations, consider these questions when researching where to stay:

- How close will you be to the slopes? If you aren't within walking distance, are you close to a shuttle route? (Remember that with small children along, you'll be carrying your equipment and theirs.)

- Does the resort offer a ski school? A two-hour lesson can make the ski experience better for each member of the family and offer valuable safety advice.

- Are your accommodations on a shuttle route to restaurants in case you want to go out?

- In case a family member doesn't take to skiing, what other activities are available nearby? (Examples: sleigh rides, a tubing hill, ice skating)

If you're driving to the resort, be sure to add the following winter safety items to your usual car emergency kit:

- Blankets
- Bag of sand or kitty litter (to spread on the ground for traction)
- Folding shovel
- Ice scraper

Cost Savers

You'll have lots of clothing and gear to purchase the first year (especially if you live in a warm weather climate). Look in advance for sales on the items you need, and buy kids' things a little big—maybe you can get two years of wear out of them. Shopping on-line can offer great deals.

Pack these accessories to make skiing safer and more comfortable:

- Neck warmer (shorter and less bulky than a scarf)
- Long underwear
- Sock and glove liners
- Hat and gloves or mittens
- Snow pants
- Goggles or sunglasses
- Hand and feet warmer packets
- Helmet (highly recommended for kids)
- Two-way radio or cell phones (for kids skiing on their own)
- Sunscreen
- Chapstick

IDEA

Rent your family's skis and other equipment at the bottom of the slope so you can easily go back in for quick adjustments and exchanges.

Whether or not frostbite is a concern depends on the outdoor temperature and wind chill. Unfortunately, by the time any telltale signs appear (like skin discoloration or feeling numb), tissue damage has already occurred. Make sure exposed areas like ears, noses, cheeks, and chins are covered. Make sure that children are wearing the same protective layers you are, like good gloves and face-protecting goggles. Ask them often if they are cold because they are likely to feel it sooner than you will.

MOM Meditations

"Your love, O LORD, reaches to the heavens, your faithfulness to the skies. Your righteousness is like the mighty mountains, your justice like the great deep" (Psalm 36:5–6). Who can look out over the majesty of the mountains and not be in awe of God's creation? Let their beauty inspire you, like the psalmist, to praise Him.

another great trip

THE
INTERNATIONAL
VACATION

The International Vacation

Travel outside of the United States offers families unique opportunities to experience different cultures and lifestyles. Kids make some of the best goodwill ambassadors and actually provide an entrée to communicating with the locals.

Spend part of the journey to your destination helping your child understand that things won't necessarily be the way they expect. When visiting another country, everyone should observe the local customs. Advise kids that eating a meal in a formal European restaurant can be an hour to an hour-and-a-half experience, and waiters in Mexico consider it rude to bring your check until you ask for it. The key is to be flexible and not get upset. If you consider language and cultural differences to be part of the fun of the trip, your children most likely will, too.

Word to the Wise: Try teaching children how to say simple phrases like "please," "thank you," and "pardon me" in the language of the country you plan to visit.

Individual passports are required for most international destinations. In order to apply for a passport, each family member must have a certified copy of their birth certificate and two passport photos taken within the last six months. An adult passport costs eighty-five dollars and a child's seventy dollars. Adolescents aged thirteen and over must sign their own passport applications. Parents may sign for children under thirteen; if both parents will be traveling with a child they must both sign the application or send a signed letter. You should allow at least a month for the processing and receipt of your passport.

Make your child's airline flight special by ordering kids' meals for the trip. You can also call ahead of time and find out what movies will be shown. Some flights to Asia and Australia even offer screens for video games. Bring along as much of your own entertainment and snacks as you can comfortably carry to help the time pass (see Appendix B).

Cost Savers

On some international flights, the cost of a child's ticket is two-thirds that of an adult's. Be sure to ask about a discount before booking the flight. (This usually doesn't apply on already-cheap fares.)

When you pack for an international trip, pack light. In most places you can wear neat, casual clothing. Frequent travelers also suggest you bring:

- A washcloth (not available in many hotels)
- Small umbrella or rain poncho
- Comfortable walking shoes and flip-flops or slides
- Lightweight sweater or wrap to cover your shoulders (required in some churches and museums)
- If your children are older, allow them to pack their own bags. You can either give them a list of things that must be included and allow them to fill in, or you can add things they miss as you "check" the bag they've packed. Bring some lightweight snacks and water bottles because you may not be eating meals on your usual schedule. Be sure to leave room in your luggage for souvenirs.

Good
IDEA

Frequent travelers counsel to keep going when you arrive at your destination. The best way to overcome jet lag is to get in sync with the local time as soon as possible and drink a lot of water. Air travel dehydrates the body.

Where are the best places to visit? Kids usually find the hustle and bustle of a city more interesting than trips through the country, even if the scenery is beautiful. Here are some favorite European destinations contributed by other moms:

* Zermatt, Switzerland: "The train ride to the town is breathtaking."

* Pisa, Italy: "We visited the leaning tower, and our boys couldn't wait to eat pizza."

* London, England: "There's so much to do in the city."

* Berlin, Germany: "The zoo is one of the best in the world."

* Europe has become much easier to travel through with the introduction of the Eurodollar. Often you aren't even required to show your passport except at the point of entry and point of departure.

Kids Can Too!

Brainstorm about how things in each country you visit are different from the United States and from one country to the next. Write down a list of everyone's observations about speech, food, transportation, scenery, and customs.

Location is the number-one factor in finding a place to stay. The most convenient accommodations will be close to the rail station, near the local metro or subway, and in the downtown shopping area. Some hotels offer junior suites, which are basically two rooms connected together, at a cheaper rate than two separate rooms. If you'll be staying in the country, bed and breakfast establishments are usually quaint, less expensive, and cleaner. Many hostels—in the past just affordable accommodations for the backpacking crowd—have become more family friendly. Visit Hostelling International's Web site at www.hihostels.com for detailed information. Always call a hostel in advance with the key questions about family suitability; you should be able to gain a sense if it's the place for your family. Many backpacker-oriented and international travel Web sites have hostel guest feedback and ratings. While hostelling can be somewhat risky, one reward is meeting so many fellow travelers from different countries.

When traveling from one city or country to another, families often opt for Eurail—the clean and timely European train system. Many different types of passes are available, including family passes. During some seasons, kids can travel free. When choosing a pass, consider that first-class passes are not much more expensive and have these benefits:

- Better availability of seating
- More comfortable seats
- A less crowded, calmer atmosphere.

Make It Memorable

Splurge on one night's accommodations in a special place like a castle, monastery, or train sleeper car. Try to schedule this treat toward the end of your trip to avoid raising everyone's expectations too early.

The same types of touristy souvenirs you find here are available in other countries. If you're looking for something unique, consider letting each child choose a Christmas ornament from the countries you visit. These can become heirlooms kids take with them to decorate their own tree when they move away from home. Let older kids select some artwork from a "favorite son" artist of the country—it doesn't have to be an original; posters are great!

great another trip

MOM Meditations

In Jesus' time, Roman citizenship carried the right to free travel and the guarantee of protection wherever a person went within the empire. You may feel hesitant traveling outside the safety of America's borders, but wherever we may live or travel in this world, our heavenly citizenship guarantees us the protection of God Himself.

THE
METROPOLITAN
ADVENTURE

The Metropolitan Adventure

Those of us who live in the country have a special fascination with the city. Most cities have their own unique personality, so visiting is rarely a case of "you've seen one, you've seen them all." Major cities are making an effort to bring people downtown by redeveloping parts of the city into venues for families.

The best way to find out what's going on around town is to contact the local chamber of commerce. You can also get information about large events in major cities from Web sites like www.citysearch.com.

Word to the Wise: Cities can be big scary places for little ones. They are packed with strange people and noises. Make sure to discuss safety protocol, and do what you can to get your little one excited about a particular event—or make a game out of the new environment.

Check out this list of metropolitan special attractions for families to enjoy:

- Zoo/aquarium/botanical gardens/planetarium

- Museums (especially children's museums and science centers)

- IMAX theaters

- Children's theater

- Downtown malls and specialty stores

- Unique restaurants

- Parks (special events abound in the summer)

- Holiday parades

- Neighborhood festivals

- Convention center events (car shows, RV shows)

- Trolley rides

Make breakfast the biggest meal of the day. Many hotels offer free continental breakfast, but even if you eat out, breakfast is a cheaper meal to splurge on than lunch or dinner.

81

Upscale downtown hotels often run unadvertised specials during less busy times of the year. If you'd like to try some first-rate accommodations, call to ask about room rates. (Lodging information you get by phone is usually more accurate and complete than over the Internet.) Not sure where to eat? Ask the concierge to help you find a restaurant your family will enjoy, and make reservations.

Kids Can Too!

Encourage critical thinking skills by giving kids a set amount of money to spend on souvenirs and other shopping. Let them decide how to allocate their funds, even if you don't agree with all their choices!

MOM Meditations

"A city on a hill cannot be hidden. . . . In the same way, let your light shine before men, that they may see your good deeds and praise your Father in heaven" (Matthew 5:14, 16). Looking out at the innumerable lights of a city, it's tempting to feel that our own contribution is small and insignificant. You don't have to be Supermom for your light to shine in the eyes of your children.

From the Trip files

For kids unaccustomed to life in the big city, be prepared to address some unexpected questions and fears. When traveling through Houston, Texas, one of our children became anxious while driving over a very high freeway overpass and finally asked, "Is this a mountain?" Before traveling to Washington, D.C., we talked excitedly about the fact that we would be riding the subway—a first for our kids. The day of our first subway ride arrived, and our youngest could hardly wait, until the subway started moving. He found the jerky motion, combined with hurtling through a dark tunnel, decidedly unnerving. It took quite a bit of convincing to get him on the subway in the afternoon for the ride back to the hotel. Then there was the time our kids wanted to know why we couldn't pick up the homeless man on the corner holding the sign "Will work for food." One of the most important lessons we've taken away from our metropolitan adventures is how city life differs from our own.

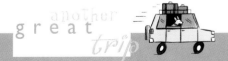

another great trip

THE
ISLAND
GETAWAY

The Island Getaway

The first image that comes to my mind when the word "vacation" is uttered is an island covered with palm trees, surrounded with white sand beaches and crystal blue water. Perhaps it can be attributed to perusing too many travel brochures, but who can resist the allure of sun, sand, and surf?

Many resorts offer an "all-inclusive" package where you don't pay extra for meals. These plans have obvious benefits, but you'll still probably save money on food and more easily accommodate your family's schedule by staying in a rented condo. Staying on the islands gives you the perfect chance to try out some food you don't usually find at home like exotic fruits and vegetables and seafood delicacies.

Word to the Wise: Island life offers a panoramic view of the culture of the island—typically from the richest excesses to the poorest of poor. Talk to your children about what they see and help them better understand our world.

For the overwhelming majority of us, an island getaway begins with a trip by plane. As one mom remarked, "This is not the time to try to read a magazine. My kids expect me to interact with them while we're in the air." Word games, like those in Appendix C, require no props and make the most of this time to reconnect. Pack all daily medications and overnight essentials (including a change of clothes) in a carry-on bag in case your luggage gets lost.

Moms often worry how kids' ears will handle the changes in pressure associated with a flight. The painful feeling that causes babies to wail on takeoff and landing is caused by a difference between the air pressure in the cabin and in the middle ear when a plane changes altitude. Those with a cold or chronic nasal stuffiness may benefit from a dose of decongestant when flying (consult your physician first). Help equalize a baby's ears by nursing her or giving her a bottle on the way up and down. Having baby suck on a pacifier also works. Older kids can chew gum, suck on a lollipop, drink something so they will swallow, and yawn to clear their ears.

Good IDEA

Bring along a stain remover stick to use on clothes that you can't launder right away.

Despite the beautiful surroundings when you arrive, there are two potential pitfalls to an island getaway:

- Kids aren't as interested in stopping to smell the hibiscus as you are;

- The number of diversions is limited by the size of the island and the activities offered.

Kids Can Too!

Often there's not a lot to do at night on an island. Before you leave home, let your children choose some quiet activities to bring along that they would like to enjoy before bed. (Examples: board or card games, activity books, Mad Libs, letter writing materials, CD player with headphones, sketchpads and art supplies, bathtub toys)

To ensure there's enough to keep everyone busy, choose an island resort with a full selection of the following:

- Nice beach
- Water-related activities like snorkeling or scuba diving
- Good pool (some families spend more time here than at the beach)
- Horseback riding
- Bicycling
- Scheduled activities for kids

another great trip

THE
TRIVIAL
PURSUIT

The Trivial Pursuit

One type of trip will hold special memories for kids—an excursion planned with their interests and hobbies in mind. The success of a trivial pursuit depends completely on your child having a good time, so arrange activities according to his or her preferences and schedule, instead of your own.

A few trivial pursuits are listed on the following pages, but the opportunities are endless. Nearly every interest or hobby has a "Hall of Fame" or a museum with a feature display of that hobby or favorite person. Finding the location can take a little ingenuity, but getting the whole family involved in the search for these spots can be fun for everyone.

Word to the Wise To get siblings excited about these hobby-oriented trips, create a calendar where they can see some possible dates available for their "trivial pursuit trip," reminding them to be flexible.

Trains

Visit a train museum where you can climb in and out of old train cars and engines. Find a large electric train display and watch until your child is ready to leave. Go to a train station and take a ride to and from a nearby stop. Visit a train shop and let your child choose a car or engine to keep.

Spelunking

Kentucky, Missouri, and southern Illinois offer miles of caverns for the caving enthusiast. In addition to guided walking tours through underground treasures like Mammoth Cave and Meramec Caverns, some caves offer spelunking tours on more challenging routes. (Bring your own gloves and knee pads!) Caving appeals to those interested in geology as well as rock climbing.

Baseball

One of our friends plans to visit all the major league ballparks in the country during his lifetime, and his kids share his passion for the American pastime. Each of his family's vacation trips is arranged through cities where they can see a game.

Ancient Civilizations

Impressive Mayan sites are found throughout Mexico and Central America. For something closer to home, explore the mounds left by Native Americans in the American Midwest.

Fishing

Our favorite fishing locale is an ocean or bay. If you're on the coast, you can fish off a pier, in the surf, or on a boat. The best thing about saltwater fishing is that you never know what you'll catch—from flounder to shark, it's always a surprise. Shallow saltwater is also the perfect place to try your hand at catching crabs. Once we "caught" a conch in a large shell that attached itself to our bait!

Theater

Is there a budding thespian, dancer, or musician in your family? Take a tour of productions on and off Broadway in New York City or the nearest major metropolitan area. Order a selection of dance, play, and concert tickets to enjoy together.

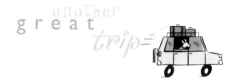

another great trip

MOM Meditations

"There is a time for everything, and a season for every activity under heaven" (Ecclesiastes 3:1). Now is the time and this is the season to nurture your family relationships. It can be as simple as sharing the experience of traveling together.

Appendix A: Toll-Free State Tourism Numbers

Alabama (AL) 800-ALA-BAMA	Indiana (IN) 800-289-6646
Alaska (AK) 800-327-5774	Iowa (IA) 800-345-IOWA
Arizona (AZ) 888-520-3434	Kansas (KS) 800-252-6727
Arkansas (AR) 800-643-8383	Kentucky (KY) 800-225-TRIP
California (CA) 800-TO-CALIF	Louisiana (LA) 800-334-8626
Colorado (CO) 800-265-6723	Maine (ME) 800-533-9595
Connecticut (CT) 800-CT-BOUND	Maryland (MD) 800-543-1036
Delaware (DE) 800-441-8846	Massachusetts (MA) 800-227-6277
Florida (FL) 888-7-FLAUSA	Michigan (MI) 800-543-2YES
Georgia (GA) 800-VISIT-GA	Minnesota (MN) 800-657-3700
Hawaii (HI) 800-GO-HAWAII	Mississippi (MS) 800-WARMEST
Idaho (ID) 800-VISIT-ID	Missouri (MO) 800-877-1234
Illinois (IL) 800-226-6632	Montana (MT) 800-541-1447

Nebraska (NE) 800-228-4307	South Carolina (SC) 800-346-3634
Nevada (NV) 800-NEVADA-8	South Dakota (SD) 800-S-DAKOTA
New Hampshire (NH) . 800-FUN-IN-NH	Tennessee (TN) 800-GO2TENN
New Jersey (NJ) 800-JERSEY-7	Texas (TX) 800-88-88-TEX
New Mexico (NM) 800-545-2040	Utah (UT) 800-233-8824
New York (NY) 800-CALL-NYS	Vermont (VT) 800-VERMONT
North Carolina (NC) 800-VISIT-NC	Virginia (VA) 800-VISIT-VA
North Dakota (ND) . . . 800-HELLO-ND	Washington (WA) 800-544-1800
Ohio (OH) 800-BUCKEYE	West Virginia (WV) 800-CALL-WVA
Oklahoma (OK) 800-652-6552	Wisconsin (WI) 800-432-TRIP
Oregon (OR) 800-547-7842	Wyoming (WY) 800-225-5996
Pennsylvania (PA) 800-VISIT-PA	
Rhode Island (RI) 800-556-2484	

Appendix B: Travel Toys

Toddlers/Preschoolers

- Etch-a-Sketch and Magna Doodle
- Number, letter, and animal-shaped magnets stored in a metal cookie tin
- Felt boards or books with felt cutouts
- Colorforms or vinyl clings to put on windows
- Small plastic action figures or dolls
- Toy telephones
- Stories on tape
- Puppets
- Pipe cleaners
- Blank pads of paper, stickers, or colored pencils

Elementary-schoolers

- Decks of cards
- Dominoes
- Assembly toys like Legos or Transformers

All Ages

- Books, books, books!

Appendix C: Word Games

Color Categories

Choose a color and have everyone help name as many different items as possible in that color.

Opposites

Call out an adjective or adverb and have your child respond with the opposite. (Examples: tall-short, hot-cold, quickly-slowly)

Mistaken Nursery Rhymes

Recite nursery rhymes and encourage your children to join in. After they are comfortable with the rhyme, change one word and see if they can tell what's different. (Example: "Yankee Doodle keep it up, Yankee Doodle Bambi...")

Guess My Tune

Take turns humming songs from Sunday school or from your child's favorite movies or TV shows. Whoever correctly guesses where the tune comes from gets to hum next.

Finish the Story

Start telling a story. With your child, take turns adding onto the storyline.

20 Questions

Get to know each other's specific likes and dislikes by asking questions about favorite and least favorite foods, places to visit, subjects in school, people you know, and more.

"The Category Is"

Choose a category like fruit, states in America, animals, or names of cars and see how many each person can name.